I0606986

George H. Woodruff

Fifty Years Ago

Or Gleanings Respecting the History of Northern Illinois

George H. Woodruff

Fifty Years Ago
Or Gleanings Respecting the History of Northern Illinois

ISBN/EAN: 9783337014353

Printed in Europe, USA, Canada, Australia, Japan

Cover: Foto ©ninafisch / pixelio.de

More available books at **www.hansebooks.com**

OR,

GLEANINGS

RESPECTING THE

HISTORY OF NORTHERN ILLINOIS

A FEW YEARS PREVIOUS TO, AND
DURING THE

BLACK HAWK WAR.

———————

BY

G. H. WOODRUFF,

AUTHOR OF "FORTY YEARS AGO," AND "FIFTEEN YEARS AGO"
CORRESPONDING MEMBER OF THE STATE HISTORICAL
SOCIETY OF WISCONSIN.

———————

JOLIET:
JOLIET REPUBLIC AND SUN PRINT.
1883.

INTRODUCTORY.

HAVING been somewhat instrumental in fixing on the 2nd day of August as the day for the Pioneers Re-union for 1882 in Will county, and in giving to the meeting a semi-centennial odor, we felt called upon to justify our course by a brief review of the events of fifty years ago, particularly as they related to this portion of Northern Illinois. Hence, the series of Historical Gleanings, which appeared in the REPUBLIC during the few weeks preceding the meeting.

It was believed that while there were a few of our older citizens to whom the events were a memory, yet the later generation were, for the most part ignorant of them, and likely to remain so, inasmuch as the accounts of them which have been preserved are scattered through various county histories, local sketches and pamphlets, which are not accessible to the general public without more trouble than most persons would be willing to take. It was thought, therefore, that it would be a good thing to gather up the facts and incidents and to weave them into a connected narrative, which would post all who desire it in the history of this region fifty years ago. Some of our friends have flattered us with the suggestion that they were worthy of re-publication in a more convenient form for preservation.

We only claim for them that they are gleanings, although considerable has been obtained by personal conversation and correspondence with living survivors, who were actors and sufferers in the events narrated. Wherever we have found a statement bearing upon the subject we have appropriated it without a scruple, giving, generally, the source of information. The first pages go back to an earlier date, but it will be seen that they lead up to the subject.

HISTORICAL GLEANINGS.

According to a tradition which we are disposed to believe, Will county was for a while the residence of a great historic character, the renowned Ottawa Chief, Pontiac. The long and bloody contest between England on the one side, and the French and Indians on the other, terminated in the treaty of peace at Paris in 1763. The most powerful ally of the French in the war for the possession of the territory included under the term New France, had been this noted Chief. He did not consider himself bound by this treaty, in the making of which the French had not consulted their Indian allies. Pontiac organized a conspiracy of the various tribes over which he was a recognized Chief, and succeeded in capturing various outposts and in butchering and stampeding hundreds of frontier families. He besieged Detroit for six months, but was defeated in his attempt to get possession of that post, and the Indians finally sued for peace, and a treaty was concluded between the English and the Western tribes in August, 1764. Pontiac, disgusted with the result of the contest, left his native region, where he had held so long and so extended a sway, and with a remnant of his Ottawa warriors— about 200 and their families—retired farther West. According to tradition, he settled on the banks of the beautiful Kankakee. There are various and conflicting traditions of his death. We gave one in " Forty Years Ago," which we found in one of the books of Western Annals, written by N. Matson, of Bureau county. According to this tradition he was assassinated by a Chief of the Illinois at a council held near the Joliet Mound, in 1769.

Pontiac was without doubt one of the most gifted and bravest of Indian Chiefs who have figured in our history. It is related of him that while carrying on the siege of Detroit, and running low in funds, he supplied his commissariat by issuing scrip made of birch bark bearing his "totem," as the only security for its redemption. It is also said that he promptly redeemed the issue—a thing which could not be said of a large amount of Michigan paper subsequently issued by white men.

This remnant of Ottawa Indians was ultimately merged in the Pottawatamie tribe, and their principal village is said to have been on the Kankakee, not far from the present city of Wilmington. It was at this village that

SHABBONEE,

an Indian who has figured largely in our more recent frontier history, was born in 1776. This was his own statement often made to different parties still living. He was born of Ottawa parents who accompanied Pontiac in his retirement to the Kankakee. Shabbonee became a Chief of the Pottawatamie tribe, by reason of the fact that he had married for his first wife a daughter of a Pottawatamie Chief named Spotka, who had a village near the mouth of the Fox river, and on his death was chosen his successor. As Shabbonee became prominent in the early history of this region, and was well known to the early settlers of this and adjacent counties, and especially because he rendered important service to the whites, his memory should be gratefully cherished, and the leading facts of his life and character should be preserved. N. Matson, Esq., of Bureau county, who was for many years well acquainted with Shabbonee, has written the most extended notice of him that we have seen. As soon as Shabbonee, at the death of Spotka, his father-in-law, became his successor, he removed his village from the Illinois river to a healthier locality on the head of Big Indian Creek, to a beautiful grove in the present limits of DeKalb county. There the tribe had their home for nearly fifty years, and the grove became a land mark known as Shabbonee's grove. It contained a fine sugar camp and a beautiful spring. The woods abounded in game, the creek in fish, while the adjacent prairie furnished rich corn land.

TECUMSEH.

In 1807 Shabbonee visited the Wabash country and became acquainted with the Shawnee Chief, Tecumseh, to whom he became warmly attached. Tecumseh, who was about seven years the senior of Shabbonee, had conceived in his mind the project of uniting all the Western tribes in a league to prevent the further granting of lands to the whites, except on the consent of the whole confederation. In pursuance of this plan Tecumseh traveled very extensively among the Southern and Western tribes. In 1810 he visited Shabbonee, as well as several other Pottawatamie Chiefs, known by the names Saug-a-nash (Billy Caldwell) Senachwine, Black Partridge, Comas and Gomo. From none of them did he get much encouragement. Shabbonee accompanied him along the Rock river and Mississippi.

In 1811 he accompanied Tecumseh to the counsel held with Gen. Harrison at Vincennes, which broke up without effecting any agreement. They then together visited the southern tribes. About two weeks after the battle of Tippecanoe they returned to the Wabash. This battle had been brought on by Tecumseh's brother, the Prophet, against his wishes, as his plans were not ripe for action.

Shabbonee, much as he loved and admired Tecumseh, does not seem to have fully sympathized with him in his plans of attacking the white settlements.

In 1812 Tecumseh sent runners along the Illinois informing the Indians of the war between England and the United States, and offering "big money" if they would take the side of England. Shabbonee intended to remain neutral, but learning that a large party from other villages, and some from his own, had left for Chicago, he mounted his pony and followed He reached there a few hours after the massacre, and his mild and peace-loving spirit was shocked at the blood and carnage there exhibited; and it was, no doubt, largely owing. to his influence, that the survivors were spared.

Late in the autumn of that year, as Shabbonee's band were about to start out on their winter hunt, emissaries from Tecumseh arrived at Shabbonee's village. They were loaded with gew-gaws so dear to the female heart, whether savage or civilized, supplied no doubt by British gold. Tecumseh had also sent the wampum belt to Shabbonee asking him to join in the war on the side of the British, and promising in their name large reward. These runners also stated, falsely, that all the bands along the river had agreed to aid him. Deceived by these statements the hunt was abandoned, and Shabbonee, with twenty-two warriors started for the seat of war. He remained in the service as an aid . to Tecumseh until the close of the war, and was by the side of the great chieftain when he received his death blow at the battle of the Thames.

There is no doubt that Shabbonee regretted having joined the side of the British in the war of 1812, and that he fully determined not to join in further hostilities against the white settlers in the West. His subsequent conduct, as we shall see, was so fully in accordance with that resolution that he came at last to be known as the white man's friend.

At the battle of the Thames there was present aiding Tecumseh also, Saug-a-nash, or Billy Caldwell, who being the son of an Irish officer in the British service, and a Pottawatamie squaw, was entitled to both an English and an Indian name. He was a man of intelligence and education, having been edu-cated by the Jesuits of Detroit; and, at the time of his death was head chief of the combined nation of Pottawatamies,

Ottawas and Chippewas. He was a Justice of the Peace at Chicago under Peoria county in 1826. Shabbonee had in his possession a paper which he highly valued being a certificate of Caldwell's given at Amherstburg (Fort Malden) in 1816, in which he certifies to the fact that Shabbonee was with Tecumseh at the battle of the Thames, and concludes by saying, "I also have been witness to his intrepidity and courageous warfare on many occasions, and he showed a great deal of humanity to those unfortunate sons of Mars who fell into his hands. [Signed,]

B. CALDWELL,
Captain I. D. (Ind. Dept.)

The celebrated Sac Chief, Black Hawk, was also present at the battle of the Thames, fighting on the side of the British.*

FOOD FOR THE NOVELIST.

In reading up the aboriginal and pioneer history of Northern Illinois, we have been struck with the abundant material it furnishes for the novelist. A series of historical romances, rivaling in interest those of Cooper, could be woven out of its veritable history, from the times of Joliet and LaSalle and the Jesuit missionaries, to the close of the Black Hawk war. From Mackinaw to the mouth of the Illinois, and westward to the Mississippi, ample room is furnished for the movement of his characters, with picturesque and interesting localities on which to exercise his powers of description—while every stream and

---

* NOTE.—Since writing the above we have received a new book of Mr. Matson's entitled "Pioneers of Illinois," in which he gives his authority for his version of the settlement of Pontiac on the Kankakee, and the place and the manner of his death. He also explaines at length the way in which the account of his death as given by Parkman and others, originated. Mr. Matson has paid great attention for many years to the aboriginal history of Illinois, and is we think entitled to thanks and credit as a careful historian.

grove, every island, mound and bluff, is rich in traditionary lore.
And then, what an endless variety of marked, peculiar, repre-
sentative characters : The first explorers and Jesuit missionaries;
the fur traders, French, English and American; Indian chiefs
and braves; dusky beauties and captive white maidens; the later
pioneers and Protestant missionaries; hunters and trappers;
saints and sinners, holy men and incarnate devils —all are waiting
to be made immortal by the pen of genius; while innumerable
wars and massacres, hunts, councils, treaties, payments, war
dances, dog feasts, pow-wows, and all the peculiar customs, super-
stitions and habits of savage and frontier life furnish an exhaust-
less fund of incident and illustration.   Have we no Cooper
among us to utilize this mine of historic wealth, and to transmute
its rough ore into the burnished gold of romance?

After the war of 1812, Shabbonee and Saug-a-nash, having
lost all faith in British promises, visited General Cass at Detroit,
and gave their formal adherence to the U. S. Government. Both,
no doubt, regretted having espoused the British side. On the
24th of August, 1816, at St. Louis, a treaty was concluded by
the United States with the Indians of the Northwest, represented
by twenty three Pottawatamie, three Ottawa and two Chippewa
Chiefs, by which these tribes ceded to Uncle Sam all their lands
lying between the Illinois and Mississippi rivers, and also a large
district west of Lake Michigan. Shabbonee was present and one
of the signers of the treaty. In 1819 this tract was surveyed
under the direction of U. S. Commissioners. Shabbonee aided
the surveyors, and with his hunters supplied the corps with game.

CASS AND THE WINNEBAGO WAR.

In July, in the year of 1827, occurred another speck of
war, called the Winnebago war, and sometimes "the
Winnebago scare." Fort Dearborn was at this time without a

garrison. It is no wonder then that the few inhabitants of Chicago were filled with alarm. Gen. Cass had gone to Green Bay by appointment to hold a treaty with the Winnebago and Menominee tribes, who failed to meet him there. He learned the cause to be a war with the whites on the upper Mississippi. He at once started on the journey around by the Fox, Wisconsin and the Mississippi rivers to St. Louis, from whence he despatched a steamer with troops to the relief of the whites. On his return by the way of the Illinois and Des Planes, he warned the settlers of their danger, and also met various Indian chiefs along the route, making them presents, and using every argument to keep them from aiding the hostiles. Among others he had an interview with Shabbonee. This Chief was heartily in accord with Gen. Cass, and used all his influence with his own and other bands to prevent them from taking the war path,

Cass spent a night at Ottawa with Dr. David Walker, and in consequence of the news he brought a fort was at once commenced on the south side of the river. Gov. Cass went on up the river and over the divide through Mud lake, and down the Chicago river, awaking the echos along its classic banks with the boat song of the thirteen voyagers, led by Robert Forsythe, the Governor's Secretary. They gave the people of Chicago the first news of the outbreak.

And here let us say, parenthetically, that this was not the Governor's first passage up the valley of the Illinois and Des Planes. In 1821, accompanied by Henry R. Schoolcraft and others, under the sanction of the U. S. Government, he made an excursion down the Wabash and Ohio and up the Mississippi to St. Louis, from which place he journeyed to Chicago for the purpose of holding a treaty with the chiefs and head men of the Ottawa, Chippewa and Pottawatamie tribes for a large tract of land in Michigan. After voyaging up the Illinois to Starved Rock they obtained horses and made the rest of the journey on

horseback. They turned aside from their route and visited the
junction of the Kankakee and Des Planes, for the especial purpose of examining the celebrated fossil tree that lies embedded
(so much as is left of it) in the Des Planes near its mouth. This
fossil is fully described by Schoolcraft in a memoir published by
him at Albany in 1822. This is one of the most remarkable
fossils ever discovered, of a vegetable origin. Specimens of it
have been widely distributed. Gov. Cass obtained several at the
time of this visit, one of which he sent to the University of
Cambridge. It has been generally thought to have been a black
walnut tree. Schoolcraft gives the size of the part exposed,
length 51. feet and some inches, and the diameter at large end,
three feet. Thomas Tousey, Esq., of Virginia, also visited this
locality in 1822 and described the fossil. From this place they
passed on over the country to Mount Joliet, and Schoolcraft wrote
the description of this Mound, which we quoted in our sketch of
the Mound.

BIG FOOT.

But we must return from this digression. One of the most
interesting reminiscences of the early Chicago is related in the
"Fergus series," by Col. Gurdon S. Hubbard, of Chicago, in
which he narrates the visit of Shabbonee, in company with Saug-
a-nash to the village of the Chief, Big Foot, at Big Foot (Geneva)
Lake. Shabbonee had reached Chicago after his interview with
Cass before him, and was the guest of his friend Caldwell. On
learning the news brought by Gov. Cass, Col. Hubbard suggested
to Caldwell and Shabbonee that they should visit Big Foot and
endeavor to learn whether he intended to join the hostiles.
From some circumstances Col. Hubbard was led to apprehend
that this Chief was unfriendly to the whites. Accordingly
Shabbonee and Caldwell at once set out on this mission. When
they arrived in the vicinity of Big Foot village Caldwell con-

cealed himself in some thick, timber, while Shabbonee entered the village. Shabbonee was at once made a prisoner and charged with being a spy. This made it evident that Big Foot was an enemy to the whites, although he had but lately returned from receiving his payment from the United States at Chicago. The situation of Shabbonee was critical. But he was equal to the occasion. He affected great astonishment and indignation at his arrest, and the suspicions against him; and claimed that he had come to consult with Big Foot in reference to joining the Winnebagoes. He avowed his conviction that the Winnebagoes were foolish and could not succeed in their schemes, and at the same time promised that if allowed to return to his people he would submit the matter to them, and if they consented he would join Big Foot. After talking all night Shabbonee was allowed to depart, accompanied by one of Big Foot's braves, to visit Shabbonee's village. As they passed the spot where Caldwell was concealed Shabbonee managed, by talking loudly to his companion, to convey to Caldwell sufficient information to guide him.

He understood at once that he must not be seen, and he returned to Chicago alone by another route. Shabbonee contrived, with consummate skill, to warn the people of Chicago of Big Foot's disposition, while his companion waited in concealment, and then the two went on to Shabbonee's village, where his people were called together, and after much talk decided not to aid the hostiles.

ALARM AT CHICAGO.   COL. HUBBARD TO THE RESCUE.

The news that Shabbonee brought to Chicago of course increased the apprehensions of the citizens, and a consultation was speedily held as to the best measures in the emergency. It was decided that Col. Hubbard should at once start for Danville for aid to defend the post, although his presence seemed equally necessary at Chicago, where most of the men were in his employ, and he had great influence with the Indians. But he was the only one well acquainted with the route and with all the settlers about Danville. He accordingly set out at once and made the journey with all possible speed, swimming the swollen rivers and riding all night. He reached the house of a Mr. Spencer, near Danville, the next day at noon, completely used up. Mr. Spencer immediately warned out the scattered settlers, appointing a rendezvous at Danville. The day following a company of 100 men, under an old frontier fighter named Morgan, was organized, and started immediately to the relief of Chicago, Col. Hubbard returning with them. Although compelled to swim the streams and wade the sloughs, they pushed on, and reached Fort Dearborn the seventh day after Mr. Hubbard had left it, to the great joy of the people. A re-organization was had, and a company, 160 strong, under Morgan, was now ready for Big Foot and all the Winnebagos.

Fortunately, at the end of thirty days, news came of the defeat of the Winnebagos, and of their forming a treaty of peace with the commanding officer of the force that Gov. Cass had dispatched by river from St. Louis. And so the Winnebago scare was at an end.

Shabbonee's course in thus counselling peace and favoring the whites gained for him the appellation of White Man's Friend. It was bestowed upon him in contempt by the hostiles, but it became his proudest title.

FATHER WALKER.

In 1823 that self-denying, earnest pioneer and preacher, Jesse Walker, received the appointment of missionary to the Indians from the Illinois conference of the Methodist Church. In pursuance of his duty as such missionary he came to Ottawa, where he is said to have built the first log cabin on the site of the present city in 1824.

More than one hundred and fifty years had elapsed since the Jesuit father, Marquette, had established his mission of the "Immaculate Conception," a few miles below that point. French sovereignty had been superseded by English, and the English again by American. Another race of Indians, too, at this time, held possession of Northern Illinois. The Illini, in the time of Marquette, so proud and numerous, had been conquered and almost annihilated by the combined Pottawatamie and Ottawa tribes, and there was hardly a vestige of the once flourishing and populous town of La Vantam, or of the Kas-kas-kia mission. The only traces of French enterprise or of Jesuit zeal were to be found in tradition and history. All Northern Illinois was still a part of the county of Fulton, and only here and there along the streams had a daring pioneer venture to build his cabin. The Indians were still in almost undisputed possession and looked upon a white man as an intruder, unless he came to buy their furs and peltries, and to supply them with trinkets, blankets, powder and hatchets, and the still more deadly "good-na-tosh."*

Elder Walker was, at the first, somewhat disheartened by his cold welcome. The Indians did not seem disposed to be friendly. One morning, while "spreading out his wants and fears before the Lord," he was surprised by a visit from a tall, finely-formed Indian, equipped with the weapons of a brave, and wearing the insignia of a chief, and whose countenance bore a kindly expression. and who introduced himself with the laconic words : "Me Shabbonee," at the same time giving the Elder a hearty hand-shake.

The chief could speak but little English and the Elder was equally ignorant of Pottawatamie, so that there could be little intelligent conversation between them. But Elder Walker was at no loss to understand that he had at last met a friend, and that his prayers were already answered; and, if he had any lingering

---

* Whisky.

doubts as to the friendly intentions of his visitor, they were soon completely removed. Shabbonee left the cabin of the Elder, giving him to understand that he would return. The camp of the Chief was about a mile distant, and he soon reappeared, bearing upon his shoulders a quarter of venison and a wild turkey, which he laid at his feet. It was a welcome addition to the Elder's lean larder. He was also accompanied by a half-breed who could speak English, and by whose help the Elder made known his objects and wishes. Shabbonee expressed his disposition to aid him.

MISSION ESTABLISHED ON THE FOX.

Accordingly next day, under the guidance of Shabbonee and George Forqua (the interpreter), the Elder explored the country along the Fox and Illinois rivers, and located his mission on a little creek that empties into the Fox, and which received the name of Mission Creek. The spot selected was on Sec. 15 of T. 35, R. 5, to which also the name of Mission Township was subsequently given. Here the earnest missionary pioneer soon had a flourishing mission, consisting of a school house, a chapel, and two or three dwellings occupied by the Elder and his assistants. Here the mission flourished for a few years, having a large school of Indian children, and a large congregation of native worshipers on the Sabbath. Many professed conversion and were baptised. Shabbonee, although heartily seconding Walker's efforts for the elevation of his people, never became an avowed convert. In 1830 the chapel was burned down and the mission was removed to the vicinity of Plainfield, where he had already started a branch. James Walker, his son-in-law, and one of his assistants, had preceded him, and built Walker's mills, famous in the early days of Will county.

From Father Walker's advent to La Salle county up to the spring of 1832, settlers "squatted" along the Fox, the Illinois, the Du Page, and their tributaries, and at a few points along the Mississippi. But Northern Illinois was still comparatively a wilderness. But it was a beautiful wilderness, consisting largely of meadow-like, flower-decked prairies, with heavy forests skirting the streams, and forming here and there island groves, breaking in upon the ocean-like monotony of the sea of verdure The country looked as if it had been cultivated in some far past, so far, that the people and their dwellings, and all vestiges of their occupation had perished. The region had only been partly surveyed, and only some canal land had been offered for sale. There were no roads, and the only pathways were the Indian trails. To this statement we must make one exception. As early as 1822 the lead mines in the vicinity of Galena had begun to be worked by white men under the protection of troops sent there by the war department, and in 1825 and 1826 there was a great rush of adventurers thither, not only from Southern Illinois, but from Tennessee and Kentucky ; not for permanent settlement but with the expectation of speedily realizing a fortune, and then returning to their homes. Many went thither in the spring and returned in the fall. Hence they received the name of suckers as their migrations synchronized with the movements of that well-known fish. The name was ultimately fastened exclusively upon the people of our State. This emigration to the lead mines had led to the opening, in 1827, of the only road in Northern Illinois, from Peoria to Galena. Along this road, at long intervals, pioneers had located for the purpose of keeping tavern in the rude style of the frontier, and soon a stage route was established between these two points.

The most important trail was that known as the Sac trail, from Rock Island to Detroit. This trail was the only guide for emigrants west of Niles, when the writer came to Joliet in 1834.

Another important trail was that from Chicago to Danville,

which came to be called Hubbard's trail, from the fact that Gurdon S. Hubbard and the men in his employ as the agent of the American Fur Company, passed back and forth upon it. He had a trading post at the crossing of the Iroquois. It was over this trail, under the guidance of Col. Hubbard, the company of volunteers went to the relief of Chicago in 1827, as we have related, and from his stores at this trading post Colonel Hubbard supplied the deficiencies of the company in arms, ammunition and rations. These supplies had been brought to that point in batteaux by the way of the Des Planes, Kankakee and Iroquois rivers. But we presume that the citizens of Watseka find it much cheaper and quicker to get their supplies by railroad. For over this identical trail now passes the Chicago and Danville, or Eastern Illinois railroad, and just across the river from the old trading post is the pleasant town of Watseka,* the county seat of Iroquois. The Indians were natural engineers, and the first pioneers good judges of town sites. Col. Hubbard ought to have a free pass over that railroad during his remaining days, which we hope may yet be many, although he has already seen more than any other man since the days of Methusaleh.

Another important trail ran from the lead mines to Big Foot Lake, and thence to Chicago. The men of wealth and taste now build their handsome summer houses upon the shores of this beautiful sheet of water, but fifty years ago Big Foot and his tribe built their wigwams along its slopes, and fished in its pellucid waters. Perhaps the savage lifted as grateful a heart to the Great Spirit for all its beauty and abundance, as does his civilized successor; and perhaps he was as happy in his frail and rude lodge as his successor, who employs architects, and skilled artisans, to construct and adorn his palatial mansion.

---

*So named from a beautiful Indian maiden, who lived thereabout ; whose interesting story we leave to the coming Cooper.

SETTLEMENTS FIFTY YEARS AGO.

At the breaking out of the Black Hawk war, fifty years ago, the largest settlement, except at Chicago, north of the Illinois river, was on Bureau Creek, where there were about thirty families. A few other settlers had located on the river at Peru and La Salle, and a considerable number at Ottawa. On Indian Creek, a tributary of the Fox, near what is now known as Munson, in the town of Freedom, La Salle county, there was a settlement known as Davis settlement consisting of eight or ten families. This settlement was soon to have a fearful history. At a place then known as Holdeman's grove, near Newark, Kendall county, there were five or six families. At Walker's Grove, or Plainfield, there were twelve or fifteen families. Along the two branches of the Du Page, partly in this county and partly in Du Page, there were about twenty families. In Yankee settlement which embraced part of the towns of Homer, Lockport and New Lenox, there were twenty or twenty-five families. Along the Hickory in the town of New Lenox, including the Zarley settlement in this township, there were probably twenty families more, and at Reed's and Jackson Grove there were six or eight more.

The humble cabins of these pioneers were, at a little distance, hardly distinguishable from the groves in whose shelter they were built, and their improvements had barely fretted the edges of the prairies that stretched in illimitable beauty before them.

NATIVE OCCUPANTS.

But these pioneers were not the only inhabitants of Northern Illinois at this time. The country between the Wabash and Rock river, and from Peoria Lake to Wisconsin Territory, was in the partial possession of, and claimed by the Pottawatamie tribe of Indians. It is impossible to state definitely their number, but including the remnants of the Ottawas that had become absorbed by them, they probably numbered not far from six thousand souls. They were divided into many villages or sub-tribes, each having its patriarchal sheik or chief, and all rendering a not very clearly defined allegiance to a head chief. All were as nomadic in their habits as the Arab, although they had attached themselves to particular localities which they claimed as specially their own, and to which they returned with some regularity. Their dwellings could be taken down, loaded on their ponies and squaws, and set up in a new spot almost as easily as the Arab's tent. These changes were as frequent as the necessities of hunting, trapping and fishing, or the manufacture of sugar, etc., seemed to require. The selling of their furs and peltries, buying the articles they needed or fancied of the traders, attending their festivals and war dances, councils and payments, etc., etc., also required frequent changes of location. They pitched their wigwams in the edge of groves and along the streams, at such points as best subserved the necessities of their mode of life, while at the same time they seemed to have been more or less influenced by the beautiful and picturesque, and, wandering as were their habits they exhibited a strong attachment to the localities with which they had grown familiar.

A strange people. They have now passed away from these scenes.

"Like the fallen leaves those forest tribes have fled.
Deep 'neath the turf the rusted weapon lies."

A remnant of perhaps 1,500 are now in the Kansas river valley and in the Indian Territory. And, while we would not excuse individual or national acts of injustice toward them, or other tribes, and while we cannot refuse a sigh of pity over their sad fate, yet one can hardly regret that these few thousand savages,

—themselves usurpers—who fifty years ago roamed and hunted over Northern Illinois, have been compelled to make room for the million or more of civilized and enterprising white men that have taken their places. Whether we call it manifest destiny, the survival of the fittest, or the working out of a divine and beneficent purpose —(may it not be all these?)—one can hardly mourn over the fact that the frail and rude lodges which were scattered up and down the streams fifty years ago, have given place to the thousands of tasteful mansions, the churches and school houses, the towns and cities, that now adorn every section of the landscape; and that the Indian trail and canoe have been succeeded by the steamers, and canal boats, and the swift-flying railway trains.

' OUR PURPOSE.

It is not our design in this historical rehash to give a narrative of the Black Hawk war in its general aspects, or of the circumstances which preceded it.

These are all amply described and related in Ford's History of Illinois and other State histories. Compared with our later war experiences, it was a very small affair. From first to last the forces of the government, including the Wisconsin volunteers, the friendly Indians, and the six artillery companies, sent forward under Gen. Scott (which took no part in the campaign), did not amount in all to much over 6,000 men. Compared with the great battles of the late war, its heaviest encounters were mere skirmishes. On the part of the Indians, there were only a few hundred at any time mustered under Black Hawk,* so that the forces brought into the field on the part of the government, would seem needlessly large. But it must be remembered that there was reason to fear that other tribes might join Black Hawk, while there was a large territory to be protected. The

---

* The best estimate we have seen places their number at 650.

Winnebagoes and Pottawattamies were not regarded as being entirely reliable in their professed friendship. It was manifestly good policy to make such a demonstration as would convince the hostiles of the futility of their designs. The advice of Polonius to Laertes is equally good for nations:

> " Beware
> Of entrance to a quarrel; but being in,
> Bear it that the opposed may beware of thee."

ROVING HOSTILES.

Besides the force under Black Hawk, there were bands of redskins roving about the country committing all those outrages in which the savage finds delight. Probably during the months of May and June, before the white forces reached the scene, there were not less than fifty of the settlers brutally murdered. From Chicago to Galena, and from the Illinois to the Wisconsin rivers, these bands scoured the country, carrying terror into every cabin.

THE WAR IN BRIEF.

The first encounter between Black Hawk's force and the whites was on the Rock river, near a stream which empties into it, and called afterwards Stillman's run, in honor of the engagement. The men engaged were raw recruits, who had at their own request been sent forward under Major Stillman to spy out the whereabouts of the enemy. They found them, May 12th, in greater numbers than they expected, and the result did not confer much glory on the volunteers. Had it occurred in the later years it would have been called a ske dad-dle. The next encounter was at Kellogg's grove, where the whites, under Major Dement were assaulted by Black Hawk's band, and the latter were repulsed with a loss of ten or fifteen of their number killed, while the loss of whites was five killed and three wounded.

The decisive engagements were fought in Wisconsin, then a part of the Territory of Michigan, whither the Indians had fled. They were pursued over the ground between the four lakes, where the city of Madison is now located, and one Indian is said to have been killed on the very spot where the capitol is built. Over this scene of beauty, (then and now), they were pursued and overtaken at the bluffs of the Wisconsin about five o'clock of the afternoon of the 21st of July, and defeated with great loss. Escaping during the night across the river; the surviving Indians made for the Mississippi, hoping to get upon the western side. But before they could accomplish their purpose they were overtaken, and the decisive battle of the war—the last encounter with hostile Indians on this side of the Mississippi was fought, August 2d, near the mouth of Bad Ax river.

According to Governor Ford's history, the best fighting on the 21st of July, had been done by the brigade of militia under Colonel Henry, and lest they might win further honors they were put in the rear on the pursuit. The result of this arrangement was, that General Atkinson with the main army was decoyed, by a small force of Indians, past the place where their main body was left in the rear, without orders. He discovered the mistake of General Atkinson, and the main trail of the Indians going down to the river, which he followed, and coming upon them attacked at once, defeating them, before the commanding General, having heard the firing, and discovered his mistake, could return with the main army.

Black Hawk, with about twenty men, succeeded in getting away, but was captured by some of his treacherous Winnebago friends at the Dalles of the Wisconsin and by them handed over to our army.

NOTABLES IN THE WAR.

Quite a number of persons played some part in the Black Hawk war whose names have since become famous.

Our own, well beloved Lincoln enlisted at the first call made by Governor Reynolds, and was chosen captain of a volunteer company, and when the first levy was disbanded, he re-enlisted as a private in the company of Captain Iles, and served to the end of the war.

He was mustered in at Dixon, where Lieutenant-Colonel Zachary Taylor was in command with two companies of regulars, by Lieutenant Robert Anderson, the hero of Fort Sumter, serving as Assistant Inspector General. At the same time there was at Dixon a young Lieutenant of the name of Jefferson Davis. It would be hard to find in all history such a meeting of persons, who were to play so conspicuous a part in their country's history, and yet who were then comparatively unknown and altogether unconscious of what the future had in store for them.

The time came when the green youth of twenty-two, the high private of Captain Iles' company, out-ranked them all.

Hon. I. N. Arnold tells us that when Major Anderson, after the evacuation of Fort Sumter, called to pay his respects to President Lincoln, after thanking him for his gallant defense, Mr. Lincoln asked Major Anderson if he remembered having met him before. The Major replied that he did not. "My memory is better than yours," said Lincoln, "you mustered me into the United States service, as a high private of the Illinois Volunteers at Dixon's Ferry in the Black Hawk war."

One coincidence relating to the arch traitor, Davis, is worthy of note. After the surrender of Black Hawk, Davis was charged with the duty of delivering him at Jefferson Barracks. The fallen chief was confined for a time at Fortress Monroe, where Davis himself was afterwards a prisoner. They were charged nominally with the same crime, that of levying war against the United States. But of how much deeper dye was the guilt of the man who had been educated at the nation's expense, and who had enjoyed its blessings and its honors, and sworn allegiance to its laws.

General Dodge, afterwards Governor Dodge, of Wisconsin, took an active part in the war. Also General Fry, afterwards our Canal Commissioner.

It was at the breaking out of the Black Hawk war that Shabbonee rendered the most important services to the pioneer settlers of this region.

SHABBONEE AND BLACK HAWK.

Black Hawk, or to give his full name as appended to the treaty of 1816, Muck-eta-me-che-ka-ka, or Black Sparrow Hawk, was at the time of the war, an old man of 72 years of age. He had been a warrior from his youth, and always bitterly opposed to the whites, especially the Americans. He was one of Tecumseh's aids in the war of 1812, and never gave in his submission to the United States Government, although he signed his X to the treaty of 1815–16, which confirmed that of 1804. He had crossed the Mississippi in 1831 with his warriors, and committed various depredations on the settlers upon the land about the mouth of Rock river—his old home—but had been met by such vigorous movements on the part of Governor Reynolds and General Gaines, of the United States Army, that he retreated to the west side, and, being threatened with pursuit by our forces he submitted, and engaged by solemn treaty to keep thereafter upon the west side. But in February, 1832, he called together a council at Indiantown, of Sac, Fox, Winnebago and Pottawattamie chiefs and head men, to which he presented his cause and his grievances, and endeavored to get them to form an alliance for the purpose of recovering from the whites the territory east of the river, where had been for so many years their villages, and their hunting grounds. The celebrated chief, known as the Prophet, was his most eloquent backer, an earnest advocate of war. Shabbonee was the principal advocate of peace. He was not much noted for oratory, but his character for honesty and good sense gave him great influence. He could also in a quiet way present his own views ably, and show the weak points in the argument of his opponent. On this occasion he gave his voice decidedly against war, urging that there was no hope of success, while hostilities on their part would only make their condition more hopeless and uncomfortable. To the high sounding statement of the Prophet, that if all the tribes would unite, they could muster a force which " would be in numbers like the trees of the forest in which they had gathered," Shabbonee replied, "True, we should be like these trees in number, but our enemies would be in numbers as the leaves upon these trees." It was no doubt the decided stand taken by Shabbonee that defeated the scheme of Black Hawk and the Prophet. Black Hawk, when a prisoner at Jefferson Barracks, said that but for him the Pottawattamie nation would have joined him.

Notwithstanding his failure to secure such an alliance as he desired, Black Hawk, as we have related, crossed the Mississippi in the spring of 1832 with the disaffected and turbulent spirits of the Sac and Fox nations, to reassert their right to the territory lying along Rock river. which had been their favorite home, and where a few miles above its mouth had been their chief town. He no doubt believed that his appearance on the war path would lead many, if not all the braves of the Pottawattamie and Winnebago tribes, to join him.

When Shabbonee heard that Black Hawk and his band of hostiles had crossed the river, he was encamped with his entire band on the Bureau, not far from the present city of Princeton. They had been engaged in the business of making their supply of maple sugar, in the manufacture of which the Indians are experts. He immediately started upon a tour among the other villages to prevent them from joining Black Hawk. For two weeks he was engaged in this mission, visiting among other places Ottawa and Chicago. At the latter place he arranged with Che-che-pin-que (Robinson) and Saug-a-nash (Caldwell) for a council to be held the following week, at a village on the Des Planes, where is now the suburb of River Side, for the purpose of agreeing upon a peace policy. The council was held, and such a policy was agreed upon, with little dissent.

. Black Hawk made one more personal application to his old comrade, and to Waubansie, to induce them to join him, but without success, and Shabbonee peremptorily refused to attend a council which Black Hawk had called, advising him to return at once to the west side of the Mississippi.

But although Shabbonee, and through his influence mainly, Waubansie and other chiefs, with their bands, refused to aid Black Hawk, there were some of the Pottawattamies from various villages, some even from Shabbonee's, that took sides with Black Hawk, and were the principal perpetrators of the outrages which soon followed.

SHABBONEE GIVES WARNING.

When the news of Black Hawk's success in that first encounter at Stillman's Run reached Shabbonee, he knew that hostile bands, encouraged by success, would soon be ravaging about the country, committing murder and every atrocity. He at once sent his son Pypegee, and his nephew Pyps, to Fox river and Holdeman's to warn the settlers of their danger, while he himself went on the same errand to Bureau and Indian creek, all starting before daylight on the 15th of May.

It was the beautiful spring season, beautiful always and everywhere, but especially beautiful then in this region, still in its pristine glory, as if fresh from the Creator's hand. The streams were mostly lined with timber, which frequently jutted out like capes into the prairie, and also here and there formed detached islands; all now in fullest, greenest leafage.   In the edges of these groves were frequent clusters of thorn and crab apple trees, and of the plum and wild cherry, now in full bloom, loading the air with fragrance, while the red bud or Judas tree and other flowering shrubs gave the grace of color to the landscape.   The hum of bees, and the song of the birds, added the charm of music to the scene, and the unbroken prairie stretched out in seas of verdure and color, filling the eye and heart with delight.

The hardy pioneers whose cabins were scattered along the edges of these groves on the Bureau, the Illinois, the Fox, the DuPage and the Des Planes, and their affluents, were busy plowing, sowing and planting, rejoicing in the fertility and beauty of the spots which they had selected for their future homes.

Over these peaceful scenes of almost paradisaical beauty, came suddenly, the startling news of savage warfare.   Shabbonee and his aids rode swiftly up and down the streams and groves giving friendly warning of the impending danger.   Leaving their plows standing in the furrows, and their cabins with whatever of goods and comforts they contained, the settlers hastened to the nearest places of refuge.

GERTY AND HIS BAND OF DEVILS.

The warning had come none too soon.   A half-breed of the name of Girty, who seems to have united in himself all the bad qualities of the two races whose blood coursed through his veins, had left the camp of Black Hawk, and with a band of guerrillas about seventy in number, which was largely composed of disgruntled Pottawattamies, coursed through the Bureau and Fox river settlements, searching for victims on whom to glut their savage cruelty.   They found that the settlers had fled.

On arriving at Shabbonee's Grove, and learning that he and his son and nephew had gone to warn the settlers of their danger,

they were greatly enraged, and denounced Shabbonee as a traitor, swearing vengeance upon him.

FIRST VICTIMS—JAMES SAMPLE AND WIFE.

Near the old Sac village, at the mouth of Rock river, a
young man by the name of James Sample had made a claim in
the fall of 1831. He had just married a beautiful girl by the
name of Lucy May. He was a local preacher of the Methodist
church, and had for two years preached occasionally at the different settlements in the vicinity of the Illinois river, Hearing of
the crossing of Black Hawk and his band, he took refuge with
the other settlers on the island where there was a fort. After
remaining there for a few weeks he concluded to go with his wife
to Hennepin, where their friends lived. As Black Hawk and his
band were supposed to be between the Rock river and the Mississippi, he thought the trip could be made with safety, although
the distance was about seventy-five miles. Accordingly they were
ferried across the river, and the young couple, well mounted,
started out on a beautiful morning about the middle of May,
hoping to reach the Bureau settlement by night, a distance of sixty
miles without an inhabitant. Their only guide was the Sac trail.
On the west side of the Bureau was a settler's cabin where they
hoped to pass the night. Their movements after leaving Rock
Island can only be inferred from well known circumstances, until
their fatal encounter with Girty's band, and the result of that encounter was related several years after by members of that band.
For a long time their fate was left to conjecture. It is known
that on arriving at the house of the settler to whom we have re-
ferred, and whose name was Henry Thomas, they found the house
deserted, and all the doors and windows barricaded as the family
had fled at the alarm given by Shabbonee's messengers. About
six miles further east was another settler of the name of Smith,

to whose cabin they would naturally go. But this was on the east side of the main Bureau creek, which at the time was very high and unsafe to cross in the darkness, which by this time would have shut down upon them, and they must have passed the night in the grove, and in the morning crossed the creek by swimming their horses. On arriving at Smith's they would be again disappointed on finding the cabin empty, and signs of a hasty flight of the inmates. Tired and hungry, and still wet from crossing the creek, the signs of the sudden flight of the settlers, which they could only attribute to fear of hostile Indians, must then have filled their hearts with alarm. But they press on. A mile further would bring them to the cabin of Elijah Epperson, on the other side of the timber, which they also found deserted. With increasing fears, which the beautiful prairie stretching out before them, and the songs of the forest angels filling the balmy morning air with music, could not dissipate, they urge on their jaded horses, when suddenly behind them they hear the terrible warwhoop, and looking back, see some twenty Indians pursuing them at full speed. As they urge on their horses they are saluted with shots from the pursuers' rifles and the deadly tomahawk flashes past their heads. Both are slightly wounded, but the attack puts new life into their jaded horses, and they soon leave the ponies of their savage pursuers far in the rear. They begin to have strong hopes of escape, when, in crossing a slough, the horse of Mrs. Sample gets mired and falls, throwing her off. Mr. Sample could still have made his escape had he been selfish enough to leave his beloved Lucy to her fate. But all the chivalry—all the manhood within him—forbids this. While assisting his wife to remount, the devils incarnate come up and surround them, with terrific, exultant yells. Sample, very inconsiderately, drew a pistol and shot one of the gang dead. The victims are quickly bound to their horses and taken back to the camp of the Indians, about a mile southeast of Epperson's.

A council was then held, and the fate of the hapless prisoners was soon fixed. In revenge for the killing of their comrade they determined that they should be burned at the stake. Sample knew Girty, the leader of the band, and offered him everything he possessed as a ransom for himself and wife. But nothing but revenge in the cruelest form could satisfy his savage nature.

We do not care to dwell upon the details of this tragedy of fifty years ago. They are minutely related in Matson's Life of Shabbonee. Suffice it to say that they were bound to a tree, and after suffering every indignity and every torture which savage ingenuity could devise, they were burned while their triumphant foes danced naked around the scene.

Early settlers afterwards noticed a burr oak standing a little out from the grove whose trunk was charred by fire, and around it they found human bones bleaching in the air, and in a ravine near by a skull. But not until many years after was it known that these were the remains in part of the youthful pair who perished among the first victims of the Black Hawk war. Within sight of this spot, where this tragedy was enacted, now lies in quiet, peaceful beauty, the city of Princeton, with its schools and churches, and its 3,500 inhabitants, the shire town of a county containing 33,000 souls.

INDIAN CREEK MASSACRE.

But the cruel murder of James Sample and lovely bride served only to whet the appetite of the savage band for blood. On Indian creek, in what is now the town of Freedom, LaSalle county, about thirty miles due west of Joliet, was a settlement of several families. William Davis had made a claim and built a cabin on the bank of the creek. He had also built a blacksmith shop near by, being a blacksmith by trade. He had commenced also to build a mill, the dam for which was nearly completed. About six miles above was the village of a Pottawattamie chief of twenty lodges. This chief, Meau-eus by name, was not particularly friendly to the whites, and took special umbrage at the building of this dam, as it interfered with the ascent of the fish to his village.

In the vicinity of Davis' cabin had settled two men of the name of Henderson, Allen Howard, William Pettigrew and Wm. Hall, all of whom had families. The settlement numbered about twenty-five souls. They had been twice warned of their danger by Shabbonee himself. Some had left for Ottawa with their families and afterwards returned. Davis was a resolute man, and determined for himself, and persuaded his neighhors, to stand their ground. They had frequently been frightened away by false alarms, and believed themselves strong enough to meet any foes that were likely to visit them.

On the afternoon of May 20, according to the narrative of Mrs. Rachel Munson (then Rachel Hall), as given in the History of LaSalle County, the situation of the settlement was as follows: H. R. Hall, the eldest son of William Hall, Mr. Davis and Mr. Robert Norris were at work in the blacksmith shop near Mr. Hall's house. Two other sons of Hall, Mr. Howard and son, two sons of Mr. Davis, and John R. Henderson were breaking prairie half a mile from the house. Henry, George and William Davis, Jr., were at work on the mill dam near by; while Mr. Pettigrew and wife and three children, Mrs. Hall and three daughters. Sylvia, aged 17; Rachel, aged 15, and Elizabeth, aged 8, and Mr. Davis, were in the house. Suddenly a band of Indians in their horrid war paint entered the dooryard and rushed for the door. Mr. Pettigrew, with child in his arms, endeavored to shut the door but was shot down. Mrs. Pettigrew, with her arms around Rachel Hall, was the next victim, the flash of the gun burning the latter's cheek. An Indian seized a child of Pettigrew's and beat out its, brains against a stump. A little son of Davis was held by two Indians while a third shot him. The deaths of Mr. Hall, Mr. Norris and of Mr. George, and of Mr. Davis and wife quickly followed. Davis was a strong, powerful man, and defended himself some time, and clubbing his rifle used it vigorously for a while over the heads of his assailants, but was at last overpowered and killed. And so the savage butchery went on until fifteen in all were killed. Some succeeded in making their escape, but only two were spared from the slaughter. These were the two girls, Sylvia and Rachel Hall.

WHY THEY WERE SPARED, AND THEIR SUBSEQUENT HISTORY.

The massacre on Indian creek was the most noted one of the war. Accounts of it are to be found in all our State, and many county histories. The most detailed account both of the massacre, and of the subsequent treatment of the two girls during their brief captivity, is given in Matson's " Life of Shabbonee," as it was obtained from one of the girls. The massacre was attended by the usual horrors of Indian warfare. The poor captive girls were compelled not only to see their parents butchered and scalped before their eyes, but to be constantly reminded of the harrowing sight by seeing the Indians, after having dressed their scalps, *secundum artem*, wear them upon their necks, when not suspended upon poles during the dance of triumph which followed the massacre, and was several times repeated. A council was held by the savages after getting to their camp, to decide upon their fate. Girty was in favor of killing them, but was overruled by others, and their lives were spared, although another prisoner, a boy of seven years, the son of Davis, was killed after going about half a mile, because he could not keep up, and his scalp was added to the horrid collection.

The reason usually given for the escape of the two girls, has been the hope of obtaining a large sum for their ransom. We shall presently give another reason which throws the only light of romance upon the dark tragedy.

The girls were mounted upon ponies, and placed each between two mounted Indians, and were taken with all speed northward, the Indians fearing pursuit from the mounted rangers. We shall not detail the circumstances attending the journey. They traveled rapidly a good share of the night, and the ensuing day, and about nine o'clock of the second night they reached the camp of Black Hawk, which was near the site of the present city of Madison, Wisconsin. From thence after some days they were taken to the camp of the Winnebago Indians on the Wisconsin, and from thence again to the fort at Blue Mounds, where they were delivered up to the commandant. Here, at the fort, they were made happy by meeting their two uncles. They were delivered up on the 3d of June, thirteen days after the massacre. Their ransom was effected by the efforts of their brother, J. W. Hall, who had escaped at the time of the massacre by jumping into the creek and hiding under the bank. Many shots were fired at him, and the Indians, supposing he was killed, did not look for him, and thus he got away and went to Ottawa, where he joined a regiment of volunteers about to march northward in pursuit of Black Hawk. He reported the case of his sisters to Colonel Gratiot, the agent of the Winnebagos, who employed two Winnebago chiefs to effect the ransom. It required the payment of $2,000 cash, forty horses, and a quantity of blankets, beads, etc., to rescue the girls.

It is, as we have said, for the hope of such ransom, that the sparing of these girls from the general butchery at Indian creek is generally attributed. But there is another fact which seems to have had a great, if not the chief weight, in inducing the band to spare them against the wishes of Girty, the leader. For this fact we are again indebted to Mr. Matson.

Belonging to the village of Meau-eaus, of which we have spoken, located about six miles above the white settlement, were two young braves named To-que-me and Co-mee. These young men were well acquainted with the settlers on the creek. One of them is said to have been a convert and baptized by the good missionary. They were frequent visitors at the Hall cabin, and each had taken a strong fancy to one of the Hall girls, both of whom were very pretty and attractive. They had made proposals to the girls' father to buy them, which is the Indian style of getting a wife. Now, as the story goes, these young braves had made it a condition, when they joined Girty's band, that the two girls should be spared. They, in common with the rest of Meau-eaus' village, were enraged at the building of the dam by Davis. Three years after they confessed to Louis Ovilmette, a half-breed, that they were in the massacre, and that it was through their influence that the girls were spared. And here we will give an episode to this affair which illustrates the strange and contradictory ingredients which are sometimes found in the Indian character.

These two young men, To-qua-me and Co-mee, were recognized by the Hall girls at the time of the massacre, and were afterwards indicted by the Circuit Court at Ottawa for their complicity in the outrage. To-qua-me was a tall, handsome youth, but his face was marked by a deep scar on his cheek, which rendered his identification easy.

For some reason the case was not brought on at that term of court, and they were allowed to go on bail given by six Pottawattamie chiefs. Before another term of court the tribe had all moved to the Indian country west of the Mississippi, the two indicted men going with them. George E. Walker, a nephew of the missionary, was at this time the Sheriff of LaSalle county, and was to some extent responsible for their forthcoming when wanted for trial. He was an Indian trader, well acquainted with the Pottawattamie language, and with Indian customs and character. A little before the term of court when their trial should come on, he went alone to the Indian country, found the refugees, and told his errand. A council of the chiefs was called, at which it was decided that the two young men must return with Walker, and stand their trial. In obedience to this decision the young men, although they expected to be convicted and executed, did not hesitate to obey, but bidding their friends farewell, set out with Walker, who traveled through the wilderness alone with his prisoners, camping with them nights, and depending in great measure upon the game procured by them, for subsistence on the way. They could easily have made their escape at any time, or could have murdered their captor.

They were put upon their trial, and were acquitted by the jury. It is probable that their course in thus voluntarily returning to stand their trial had made a favorable impression upon the jury. Besides this, they were not identified by the Hall girls very fully. To-qua-me had taken the precaution to avail himself of his Indian right to paint, and had done it so skillfully that the scar upon his cheek did not show, and consequently the girls could not swear positively to his identity, and it may be that the girls were not altogether untouched with pity for their old admirers. This is a surmise which we make for the benefit of the coming man, or woman, who shall weave a thrilling romance from the incidents of our early history.

There may be some who would like to know the subsequent history of the two girls.

The Legislature, at their next session, voted each one a donation of land from the canal tract, and it is related in the history of LaSalle County that Congress voted a donation of money. Rachel Hall was married in March, 1833, to William Munson, Esq., of LaSalle county, and they became comfortably wealthy. She died in 1870. Before she died she placed a monument over the graves of the victims of the massacre. She lived near the scene of the tragedy. Sylvia Hall was married in May of the same year to Rev. William S. Horne, who, so far as we know, is still living at Lincoln, Nebraska. In 1833 she and her husband sold to James McKee, Esq., then of Jacksonville, the " float " to an eighty of canal land, which he located on the w $\frac{1}{2}$ of s e $\frac{1}{4}$ of s 9; which piece of land had the good fortune to lie on the west bank of the then humble and obscure, but now famous, historic, classic and fragrant Des Planes river, and which became West Joliet.

There were several other murders of settlers in this vicinity and on the Bureau, but we will not stop to particularize them.

WHISKY AND TOBACCO.

We return to our narrative of events. When the alarm was given to the settlers on Fox River, by Pyps, the nephew of Shabbonee, they at once fled in the direction of Walker's Grove (Plainfield.) Among the fugitives was one Clark Hollenbeck, who kept a store on Fox river, not far from what is now York-ville, Kendall county. The two principal articles of his stock in trade were whisky and tobacco. Of course he had to leave every-thing behind. And here occurred a notable instance of the good which these commodities, against which fanatics declaim so much, can do. If it had not been for this whisky and tobacco of Hollen-beck's, it is beyond doubt the settlement at Walker's Grove would have shared the fate of the one on Indian creek. For when Girty's band entered the store and found the whisky and tobacco, they could not resist the temptation to stop and have a big drunk and a big smoke. So, instead of pursuing the fleeing settlers, they turned out their ponies to grass and spent the night in a drunken pow-wow. This gave the fugitives time to reach the DuPage and warn the settlers in the vicinity of Walker's Mills. Yes, it was Clark Hollenbeck's whisky that saved the pioneers at Walker's Grove from massacre; and yet, such is the ingratitude of men!—the good people of Plainfield are bitterly opposed to whisky, and Father Beggs, who would no doubt have had his scalp lifted but for it, loses no opportunity to denounce it!

And here we have to relate another incident of the flight which illustrates the strange and contradictory elements of the Indian character : Among the settlers on the Fox river was a Mr. Harris, who, with his sons, was absent hunting their horses at the time the warning came, and the rest of the family left on foot with the Aments and Clarks from the same vicinity. But the father of Mrs. Harris, Mr. Combs, was an old man, and at this time he was entirely disabled by an attack of inflammatory rheumatism. It was a terrible quandary for Mrs. Harris and her neighbors. But Mr. Combs solved it by saying, "Flee, and leave me to my fate; I am an old man and have but a little while to live at best." There was no other way to do but leave him, or stay and perish with him. Soon after Mrs. Harris and children had gone, the cabin was entered by a party of Indians, showing that they went none too soon, although they left their supper upon the table, untouched. The Indians, however, did full justice to Mrs. Harris' cuisine. Mr. Combs, who, of course expected to be killed at once, was surprised to find himself treated with kindness. The Indians administered to his wants during the three or four days they remained in the neighborhood; so that when the place was visited a few days after by a company of rangers he had improved in health, and was able to be taken to Walker's Grove.

It is probable that the Indians regarded a man prostrated by disease with a kind of superstitious reverence; or, they might have thought that a man suffering under inflammatory rheumatism was already tortured beyond their power to add any thing to his torment.

The appearance of the fugitives, some on foot, some on horseback, and some in wagons, some bareheaded and barefooted, and crying out "Indians! Indians!" was the first notice that the settlers at Walker's Grove and vicinity had got of their danger. The consternation produced can better be imagined than described. The leading men in the settlement hastily consulted together as to the best course to be adopted. Some were for flight in one direction or another. It was concluded that the best course, at least for the present, was to get together and make a defense. The cabin of Father Beggs, on section 16, was thought the best one for the purpose, and accordingly, they gathered there and hastily put it into the best condition to resist attack. By common consent James Walker, a man of great energy and good judgment, was made generalissimo. Barricades were erected by tearing down fences and out-buildings, and they soon had a stronghold which became known as "Fort Beggs." Everything that could be of service as a means of defense, such as axes, pitch-forks, etc., were collected and brought to the fort. The women made themselves useful in melting up their stock of pewter ware—more valuable then than silverware now—and running musket balls. Only four guns, however, could be mustered that could be relied upon. Here they remained in anxious suspense for several days expecting every moment to hear the yells of savage foes coming to attack them.

The following families and person were living in this vicinity at this time: *

Jesse Walker, the pioneer missionary, and family; James

---

* We are mainly indebted to Father Beggs, who still lives, for this list.

Walker and family; Reuben Flagg and family; Timothy B.
Clark and family; Rev. Stephen R. Beggs and family; John
Cooper and family; Chester Smith and family; Wm. Bradford
and family; Peter Watkins and family; Samuel Shively and
family; Thos. R. Covel and family; James Matthews and family;
Mr. Elisha Fish and family; Rev. Wm. See and family; Ches-
ter Ingersol and family; James Gilson and family; Robert W.
Chapman, James Turner, Orrin Turner, John Shutleff and
Jedediah Wooley, Sr.

These, with the fugitives from Fox river, made the number,
old and young, gathered in Fort Beggs, one hundred and twenty-
five. As may be readily imagined the cabin was uncomfortably
full.

While here, expecting every hour to be attacked, their fears
were greatly increased by the visit of a man named Lawton, with
some friendly Indians, who reported the country full of hostiles
and advised the people in the fort to leave at once for Chicago,
He made but a brief stop, he and his company hurrying on to
that place.

The people of Chicago, hearing of the exposed position of
the settlers on the Du Page and the Fox rivers, had hastily organized a company of volunteers to go to their relief. It consisted
according to most accounts of twenty-five or thirty mounted
men. Some accounts say it was under command of Captain
Naper, of the Naperville settlement, while others say it was commanded by Captain Sisson, from the Yankee settlement, and in
other accounts it is spoken of as Captain Brown's company. It
is probable that all these persons were along, and being active
men in getting it up, were all captains. We know no other way
to reconcile the different statements. The writer knows from
personal conversation with Mr. Sisson, that he was with the company. At the same time Lawton, above named, a man who had
settled on the Des Planes, near the present village of Riverside,

and who was well acquainted with the Indians, and had a squaw for a wife, with about the same number of friendly Indians accompanied the mounted rangers. They stayed the night of the 21st at Lawton's place, and on the next morning Lawton and his company started for the Big Woods settlement, near the present town of Aurora, where there was at the time an encampment of Pottawatamies. The rangers struck for Holderman's. They agreed to meet at the cabin of George Hollenbeck. The company arrived at Plainfield and stayed over night and then proceeded on to Holderman's grove. They met Cunningham and Hollenbeck on the way who informed them of the destruction of their property, telling them it was useless to go farther. Notwithstanding this, they went on to Holderman's, and stopped over night, from whence they sent an express to Ottawa to notify the settlers of the safety of their property. This express returned early next morning with the news of the massacre on Indian creek. They then went to Ottawa and from thence to the scene of the bloody tragedy, where they collected and buried the remains. The scene presented was horrid beyond description. While the company was engaged in this painful duty, Lawton, after going to the Big Woods, had gone to the cabin of Hollenbeck, where, instead of meeting the rangers, he found himself in the company of a hundred hostile Indians, who took him prisoner and threatened to kill him, but his relations with and knowledge of Indian character served him a good purpose. He had old friends in the crowd who effected his liberation, when he and his companions hastened with all speed for Fort Beggs, reaching it with the news as before stated. He supposed that the company of rangers had been all butchered.

The visit of Lawton greatly increased the excitement and consternation at the Fort. Father Beggs says : "The stoutest hearts failed them, and strong men turned pale, while women and children wept and fainted." The first impulse of most was to seek safety in flight. But this might be jumping out of the frying pan into the fire. Mrs. Flagg, a woman of great judgment and resolution, strongly supported those who thought it best to "hold the Fort." To this decision, most fortunately, they came. It was afterwards ascertained that there were Indians lying in wait for them. They made what preparations they could to meet the attack of the redskins. They built bon-fires and kept them burning around the Fort all night, so that the approach of the enemy could be seen. On the second day after Lawton's visit the rangers put in their appearance on their return, bringing the news of the Indian creek massacre and other outrages. It was then unanimously concluded to go under the protection of the rangers to Chicago. It is a tradition that a party of Indians were lying in wait for them at Flagg creek, but seeing they were so well protected did not venture to attack.

FATE OF PAYNE—ANOTHER VICTIM.

Of the incidents and experiences of the refugees at Chicago we will speak bye and bye. There was one man who had taken refuge in the Fort for a night from Chicago, who, when the settlers left, as related, also left Fort Beggs, but in another direction. This man was Rev. Adam Payne, a preacher something after the independent style of Lorenzo Dow, and who is said to have been a man of great piety, earnestness and eloquence. He was on his way from Chicago to some place in Putnam county where his family resided. He was strongly urged to return to Chicago with the rest. But this he declined to do. He had been with the Indians a good deal, and preached to them often, and numbered some of them among his converts. It is said that Simon Girty had sometimes acted as his interpreter. He was a man of commanding and reverend appearance, tall and finely formed, wearing his hair and beard very long. He was well mounted, and being armed with a spy-glass by which he could discover an Indian at a great distance, he thought he might safely proceed to his destination. So when the citizens and rangers left Fort Beggs for Chicago, he started for Ottawa.

That his confidence was unwarranted was afterwards apparent. His body, mutilated of the head, was found a day or two after by a company of mounted rangers, among whom were Gurdon S. Hubbard and George Walker, about five miles northwest of Marseilles, and by them it was buried. It was identified by his bible, spy glass and pocketbook, with a sum of money. These articles having for some reason escaped the notice of his murderers, they were sent to his family. It is a tradition that the Indians had taken his head as a trophy and performed their war dances about it, and that Girty, who was not with the party that murdered him, when he recognized the face of Payne, was very much grieved over the affair, and had it buried. .

ON THE DUPAGE.

While these events were transpiring at Walker's Grove and elsewhere, as we have related, a similar state of things was transpiring in the settlements on the DuPage. There were two settlements, one on the east and one on the west branch. That on the east, including the junction, is now embraced in Will county, and the other about Naperville in DuPage county. Of course at the time both were included in Cook county. On the east DuPage were the families of Pierce Hawley and wife, Stephen J. Scott and wife, Willard Scott and wife, Walter Stowell and wife, Israel P. Blodgett* and wife, Rev. Isaac Scarrett and wife, Harry Boardman and wife, Robert Strong and wife, Seth Wescott and wife, Lester Peet, and a hired man at Hawley's and another at Boardman's.

---

*Father of Judge Blodgett, of Chicago.

Up the west branch was the Naper settlement, probably embracing about the same number of settlers. Among these were the families of Baily Hobson, Uriah Payne, Capt. Joseph Naper, John Naper, H. T. Wilson. Lyman Butterfield, Ira Carpenter, John Murray, R. M. Sweet, Alanson Sweet, C. Foster, J. Manning, H. Babbit and others.

The startling news, that Black Hawk was on the war path, and they were in danger from hostile bands, was brought to their settlement by Shata, an express from the Potttawatamie village at Big Woods. There was of course the same excitement and alarm that obtained at Walker's Grove. Chicago presented the nearest haven of refuge, and thither the settlers went as soon as possible, with such means of conveyance as they could command, arriving at Chicago the 20th of May. The families remained in Chicago, mostly at the Fort, for some weeks, with the refugees from other settlements. Several excursions, however, were made by the men to their homes to look after matters, and ascertain the state of the few crops that had been planted. Among others, the company of which we have spoken, who went to Plainfield by the way of Naperville.

FORT PAYNE—ANOTHER VICTIM.

A short time after, also, Capt. Jo Naper, Capt. Harry Boardman, and about a dozen others, after going from Chicago to the settlement, kept on to Ottawa to get assistance from Gen. Atkinson to build a fort. They succeeded in getting an order from Gen. Atkinson for a company of men stationed at Joliet, as we shall hereafter relate, to go to Naperville. They built a fort near the present residence of Lewis Ellsworth, which they called Fort Payne, in honor of the Captain. It was a stockade with two block houses. While the Fort was building an incident occurred which showed its necessity. Two men, named Brown and

Buckley went to Sweet's Grove to obtain a load of shingles. While on the way, and near the Grove, Buckley got out of the wagon to open the fence; Brown drove through and on, while Buckley followed leisurely behind. Suddenly Buckley heard the sharp report of a rifle and saw his comrade fall dead from the wagon. Greatly alarmed he turned back and fled toward the settlement, reaching the Fort with hardly strength enough to tell the story. About twenty men started out to the scene of the disaster. They found that the horses had been carried off, and the body of Brown was pierced with three balls. It was taken to the Fort and buried. Many of the men had returned to the settlement and occupied the Fort, and made occasionally excursions into the surrounding country. Of course Capt. Joseph Naper was the leader in all such scouts. Willard Scott, who is now a resident of Naperville, was also one of the most reliable men in the emergencies of the time, having a thorough knowledge of Indian character, great influence with them, and a thorough frontiersman. Serious as was the condition of affairs it did not prevent the men from indulging in some practical jokes. Such men as Jo Naper, Harry Boardman, Robt. Strong and Willard Scott, could not be repressed for a great while at a time. Among other stories of the period we copy the following from the history of DuPage county.

" About this time Messrs. Hobson, Goodwin, Boardman and Strong, were returning from Chicago with two ox teams. Hobson and Goodwin were riding in one wagon, and Boardman and Strong in the other. It was a warm summer's day, and Strong laid down in the wagon and fell asleep. Discovering that his companion was taking a nap, and ever on the *qui vive* for a little fun, Boardman called to Hobson to come and fire his gun near Strong's head and see what the effect would be. Hobson did as directed, when Strong suddenly awakened by the report, and supposing himself beset with Indians, made a desperate attempt to go down through the bottom of the wagon box. The joke was now on Strong, and after the laugh had subsided they drove on. Bye and bye, Strong concluded to try Hobson's courage A plan was secretly devised between him and Goodwin, by which Strong was to secrete himself in a thicket some distance ahead, and when Hobson came along, get up some demonstrations that would lead him to think there were Indians there. As Hobson's team approached the place the war-whoop was sounded and one or two shots were fired. Goodwin manifested extreme terror, and seizing both guns ran off, leaving Hobson alone with nothing to defend himself with but an ox gad. But he was not much intimidated, and, without altering his course, rode past the thicket, standing erect in his wagon, with a fixed and searching look upon the place from which the manifestations proceeded. Strong abandoned the idea of attempting again to frighten Hobson, and Goodwin was coolly informed that if he ever meddled again with Hobson's rifle he would be in danger of getting the contents through his own head."

Mr. Strong and his wife still survive the dangers of that day and of the intervening fifty years as well, and if this story is not correctly reported he can give his version on the 2nd of August next, when we hope to see him and all other survivors of the Sauk scare at the pioneers' picnic at the Joliet-Fair Grounds.

During the period we are reviewing a company of mounted rangers was organized at the settlement of which we will give the muster roll bye and bye, with others organized at Plainfield and Yankee Settlement.

YANKEE AND HICKORY SETTLEMENTS.

The alarm was carried to the "Yankee" and "Hickory Creek" Settlements by Hiram Pearson, of Chicago, and Daniel Mack, of Hadley, who had started for Danville and encountered fugitives from the west, somewhere near the DesPlanes river.

They returned at once and gave the alarm. Most of those in Yankee Settlement fled to Chicago, while those on the Hickory and in the groves along the DesPlanes and on Jackson creek sought safety at Danville and on the Wabash.

There were residing then in Yankee Settlement, including in that name Homer and Lockport, and part of New Lenox, the following men, most of whom had families :

Benjamin Butterfield, Thomas Fitzsimmons, James Glover, John McMahon, Joseph Johnson and two sons, James Ritchey,* Edward Poor, Joseph and James Cox, John Helm, Salmon Goodenow, Joseph McCune, Selah Lanfear, Peter Polly, David and Alva Crandall, Uriah Wentworth, John Blackstone, John Ray, Mr. Ashing, Mr. McGahan, Armstead Runyon, Holder Sisson, Calvin Rowley and Oren Stevens.

On the Hickory, from the DesPlanes to Skunk's Grove, were the following, most of whom had families :

Reason Zarley, Philip and Seth Scott, Robert G. Cook and father, Wm. Billsland, Daniel Robb, Jesse Cook, Robert Stevens, David Maggard, John Grover, Isaac and Samuel Pence, Thomas and Abram Francis, Aaron Ware, Wm. Gougar and sons. Joseph Norman and son, Judge Davidson, Lewis Kercheval and son. Aaron Friend, Rufus Rice, James Sayers, Michael Runvon. Wm. Rice, John McGovney, Wm. Osborn, C. C. Van Horn and Abram Van Horn and Henry Watkins.

In Jackson and Reed's Groves were Charles Reed, Joseph and Levi Shoemaker, George and John Kilpatrick, James Hemphill, Wesley Jenkins, Charles Coons, Jefferson Ragsdale, Henry and George Linebarger and sons, Charles Longmire and Daniel Height, most of them having families.

Most of the settlers on the Hickory and in the groves we

*Still living.

have named sought safety in flight toward Danville and on the Wabash. The same terror and excitement prevailed, and they left in haste, taking but little with them, save the clothes they had on. Some ludicrous scenes used to be related by some of the participants in the stampede. The narrators perhaps "drew a long bow," and we will not repeat the stories.

On their way toward Danville they met the detachment of four companies of rangers, and some of them turned back under their protection.

When the report of Indian hostilities and outrages on the Fox, DuPage and DesPlanes rivers reached Danville, Hon. Gurdon S. Hubbard, then residing there, pursuaded Col. Moore, who commanded the Vermillion county militia, to call out his regiment for the scene of war without waiting for orders from the Governor. At his own expense Mr. Hubbard bought provisions and ammunition, and also furnished transportation wagons. The news was received on Sunday. By Tuesday the detachment marched with rations for ten days, arrangements being made for more to follow. They reached the DesPlanes river at the point now known as Joliet. They commenced at once to build on the highest point of the bluff overlooking the river on the west side, on ground now occupied by the residences of Frank Marsh and Charles C. Russell, a stockade with a block house. Mr. Hubbard reported to Gen. W. Atkinson at his headquarters below Ottawa, by whom he was directed to leave one company to complete and garrison the fort, and to report with the rest of the regiment at his headquarters, which was done immediately.

Among those who turned back from their flight were Jesse Cook and Reason Zarley and his family. They assisted in the building of the stockade, and Zarley and his family remained in it some three weeks, until the company left.

Joseph Naper, of the Naper Settlement, had applied to Gen. Atkinson for assistance to protect his settlement, and had succeeded in getting an order for its transfer to that point. For this act Mr. Zarley never forgave Capt. Jo Naper. Our "Cal" was then a lad of about nine years of age, and remembers very distinctly the residence at Fort Nonsense, (as it was called) and also of seeing a company of friendly Pottawatamies, who had encamped under the bluff about the old McKee spring. So that fifty years ago, the spot from whence we are writing these gleanings, was an Indian camp.

The Vermillion regiment was soon disbanded, and Col. Hubbard joined a spy company, composed of officers and Indian fighters, for sixty days. Mr. Zarley and family, after stopping a while at the Sisson Fort, again took up their retreat for Danville, where they remained until the trouble was over, and while there James C. was added to the family.

Robert Stevens and David Maggard also returned and made a private stronghold in a rocky ravine which then existed in the bluff opposite the present paper mill, and which was concealed from sight by a thick growth of red cedar and other shrubs and vines.

AT CHICAGO.

Having conducted the fleeing settlers from various localities to Chicago, it is time that we should turn our attention to that point and see what kind of a "Zoar" it proved to be. Like the city where Lot found refuge, it was then chiefly noted for its smallness. Besides the Fort and its barracks, and the light house, there were but five or six buildings, mostly log huts, on all that ground now covered by immense business blocks and palace hotels. Of course such a place could but very poorly accommodate the families that fled thither. Fort Dearborn had been evacuated by an order of Gen. Macomb, issued in 1831, and, although in February, 1832, he had issued an order that Major Whistler, of the 2nd Infantry at Niagara, on being relieved at that place, should repair with the troops under his command to Fort Dearborn at Chicago, yet he did not arrive until the 17th of June. Consequently the Fort and barracks were unoccupied by a garrison at the breaking out of the war. The fugitives there-fore mostly found a refuge in the quarters at the Fort, but it was so crowded as to be very uncomfortable. Father Beggs says: "Two or three families of our number were put into a room fifteen feet square, with as many more families, and here we stayed crowding and jamming each other for several days."

But this was not the only trouble. In their hasty flight most of the settlers had hardly thought of the matter of supplies, and little or nothing was to be found in Chicago, so that it seemed as though the choice was between being scalped or starved. Archibald Clyburne had been contractor to supply the garrison with beef and also for the Pottawatamie Indians, and from him some relief was obtained.

Father Beggs relates, in his book, two startling incidents, which added greatly to the misery of the situation. The first was a severe thunder storm, during which one end of the room, in which he and others were quartered, was struck by lightning, the fluid passing down through a room below, in which was a keg of powder within a few inches of the track. The other incident or incidents we give in the Elder's own words: "The next morning our first babe was born, and during our stay fifteen tender infants were added to our number. One may imagine the confusion of the scene—children were crying and women were complaining within doors, while without the tramp of soldiers, the rolling of drums, and the roar of cannon added to the din." No words of ours could add anything to this graphic statement.

The soldiers at this time must have been the volunteer organizations that had been formed for defense before the arrival of the regulars.

There is still extant a muster roll of the organization of the citizens formed early in May on the first alarm. We copy it entire from one of the Fergus pamphlets :

"May 2, 1832.—We, the undersigned, agree to submit our-selves, for the time being, to Gholson Kercheval Captain, George W. Dole and John S. C. Hogan, First and Second Lieutenants, as commanders of the militia of the town of Chicago, until all apprehension of danger from the Indians may have subsided :"

Rich I. Hamilton, Jeddiah Woolley, Jesse B. Brown, George H. Walker, Isaac Harmon, A. W. Taylor, Samuel Miller, James Kinzie, John F. Herndon, David Pemeton, Benj. Harris, James Gindsay, S. T. Gage, Samuel Debaif, Rufus Brown, John Wellmaker, Jeremiah Smith, Wm. H. Adams, Herman S. Bond, James T. Osborne, Willian Smith, E. D. Harmon, Isaac D. Harmon, Charles Moselle, Joseph Lafromboise, Francis Lebarque, J. W. Zarley, Michael Ouilmette, Henry Boucha, Christopher She-daker, Claude Lafromboise. David McKee, David Wade, Ezra Bond, William Bond, Robert Thompson, Samuel Ellis.

This must have comprised nearly all the abled-bodied citizens of Chicago at the time, and of this number some were from outside. Jeddiah Woolley and J. W. Zarley were from our terri-tory; the last named being the oldest son of Reason Zarley, and George H. Walker belonged in Ottawa.

When we remember that only twenty years before Chicago had been the scene of a most brutal massacre, in which the Pottawatamie Indians had joined, we cannot wonder that the few settlers there, in the spring of 1832, were filled with alarm, and that they looked anxiously for the arrival of Major Whistler and his command. On June 17th they arrived, but their arrival, much as it had been desired, was not without its disadvantages. He demanded posses-ion of the government barracks for the use of his own family and officers. Father Beggs says : " The

Major and his family came into our room and we were turned
into the pitiless rain storm that afternoon. We found shelter in
an open house, where, from the dampness and exposure, Mrs.
Beggs and the child took a severe cold. Col. Hamilton then
gave us the use of one of his small rooms."

The history of DuPage county says : "When the regular
troops came on from Michigan the settlers were ordered to quit
the Fort, and every hovel that would afford a shelter was immediately crowded with occupants. At this time there were several
women and children in the Fort, whose husbands and fathers
were at Naper Settlement, building the fort there. These would
have been turned out of doors had it not been for the entreaties
of the volunteer company. By an exceedingly liberal provision
Mrs. Hawley and six children, Mrs. Blodgett and four children,*
and Mrs. Hobson and five children, were allowed to occupy an
upper room in the establishment, about ten feet square."

Such was the uncomfortable position of the fugitives in
Chicago that many preferred to return to their homes and take
the risk of Indians, and as time passed, and the Indians
seemed to have left the vicinity and the cloud of war was passing
north and west, their apprehension in a great measure subsided.

ARRIVAL OF GENERAL SCOTT AND THE CHOLERA.

On the evening of the 10th of July Gen. Scott arrived at
Chicago. Four steamers had been chartered by the government
for the transportation of troops and supplies to Chicago. At this
time no steamers had ever plowed the waters of Lake Michigan,
and from Mackinaw to Chicago there were no light-houses, no
beacon lights, no piers or wood stations, and the few natural
harbors were unimproved. At Chicago a sand bank prevented
the ingress, of any craft that drew over two feet of water, the
mouth of the river being then as far south as Madison street.

* One of these children is Judge Blodgett, of Chicago.

The steamers chartered by the United States were the Henry Clay, Superior, Sheldon Thompson and William Penn. On the voyage the cholera broke out among the troops and crews on board these vessels so violently and fatally that two of them were were compelled to abandoned the voyage, proceeding no further than Fort Gratiot, at the entrance of Lake Huron. The scene on the Henry Clay was especially terrible. All discipline was at an end. As soon as the boat reached the wharf every man sprang ashore, and sought refuge in the woods, and some lay down in the streets, and under cover of the river bank and died unaided and alone. On the Sheldon Thompson, one of the boats which came on, the disease did not break out until after passing the Manitou Islands, but before reaching Chicago thirteen were committed to the waters of Lake Michigan. Three more died during the night making sixteen. In the course of the next day and night eighteen others died and were buried near the corner of Lake street and Michigan avenue. In the four following days fifty-four more died, making an aggregate of eighty-eight. These facts are related by Capt. A. Walker, commander of the Sheldon Thompson, which reached Chicago July 10th, the first steamer that had ever anchored off Chicago. She carried Gen. Scott and staff and troops, who were landed in yawls. The William Penn with troops and military stores arrived a week later.

No language can describe the alarm and distress produced by this arrival, which had been so ardently hoped for. All were as anxious to escape from Chicago as they had been a few weeks before to get there. This was the first visitation of cholera in the United States, and the terror which the mere name then produced cannot be imagined.

This outbreak of cholera of course, for a time, delayed the advance of Gen. Scott. On the 20th of July he moved his camp to the DesPlanes river, hoping that the change would be

for the benefit of his men. His camp was founded on the ground
now occupied by Riverside. Leaving Col. Cummings in command he, with twelve men and two baggage wagons, started in
advance. He ordeded Col. Cummings to advance as soon as the
health of the troops would admit. The train of wagons and
horses had been brought overland from Ohio, where they were
purchased. Other men and teams from the surrounding country
were pressed in the service. Selah Lanfear and his team from
Yankee Settlement was among the number so employed, and one
of the teamsters was a lad of seventeen of the name of Robert
N. Murray, the son of a settler at Naperville. This lad is now
the Hon. Judge Murray of DuPage county.

Col. Cummings, with the main body of Scott's forces, started
on in about ten days, and had reached the present site of Beloit,
on Rock river, when the news of the battle of Bad-Ax was brought
to them with orders to move to Rock Island.

At this point the cholera again broke out among the troops
that had gathered there from various points, including the rangers or volunteer companies that had been organized. Here Gen.
Scott displayed as great heroism as in the battle-field. He fear-
lessly exposed himself in his attentions to the sick, both privates
and officers, showing the utmost kindness while, at the same
time, enforcing the most rigid sanitary regulations. Four officers
and about sixty men were the victims of the scourge at this point.

As may readily be imagined the arrival of Gen. Scott with
the cholera produced a stampede of the settlers *from* Chicago
quite as sudden and as hasty as the one produced a few weeks
before by the alarm of Indian outrages *to* Chicago. Fort Dearborn, although now garrisoned, was no protection from the
enemy which had crossed the ocean and which travelled everywhere, without any regard for quarantine regulations or State or
army lines.

John Watkins, the well-known ancient pedagogue, and who is now a resident of this city, tells us that when Gen. Scott sent word from the steamer that he was going to land, he thought he would rather risk the Indians than the cholera, and he started for his father's, Henry Watkins, on Hickory creek. But on arriving at his father's cabin he found it empty, the family having gone to the Wabash with the settlers in that vicinity. He then turned his face once more for Chicago, but on his way he met Col. Hamilton and Gen. Brown, who, notwithstanding their high military titles, were fleeing from this new enemy. They reported such a fatality among the troops that he joined them in their flight to Danville.

After the alarm was over he returned to Chicago and opened his school. His name appears as one of the witnesses to the Indian Treaty of 1833, and he is one of the few remaining survivors of that period.

EARLIEST WAR RECORD OF WILL COUNTY.

Many of the settlers had already ventured to return to their locations. Besides the two forts we have already named a block house was built in Yankee Settlement on the Sisson place, and the men placed themselves under the command of Holder Sisson, a soldier of the war of 1812.

Many of the settlers also returned to Walker's Grove and Napier Settlement, and looked after their crops and farm work during the day, and found refuge in the block houses at night.

Capt. Joseph Naper was in command at the block house in Napier Settlement, James Walker at Walker's Grove, and Holder Sisson, at Yankee Settlement.

A company of mounted rangers was organized at each of these three localities, and they were duly mustered into the United States service, and they would, unquestionably, have made a brilliant military record if they had had an opportunity. They each one, no doubt, drew their land warrants.

We give the muster roll of each of these companies, taken from the Adjutant-General's office at Washington.

Muster roll of a detachment of mounted volunteers, commanded by Captain James Walker, enrolled June 25th, 1832, in Cook county, Illinois, and mustered out of service August 12th, 1832:

James Walker, Captain.

Lieutenants—First, Chester Smith; Second, George Hollenbeck.

Sergeants —Wm. See, Edmund Weed, Chester Ingersoll.

Corporals—Elisha Fish, Reuben Flagg, Peter Watkins.

Musician—Edward A. Rogers.

Privates—B. F. Watkins, Henry Jones, Thomas Woolley, Henry Weakley, Ralph Smith, Elisha Curtiss, Samuel Fountain, Thomas R. Covell, E. G. Ament, Peter Watkins, J. Woolley, A. C. Ament, James Gillson, Hiram Ament, D. J. Clark. Total, 25 men.

Rev. S. R. Beggs was also a member of this company, but being detained in Chicago, his name was not on the muster roll, but he got his land warrant.

Muster roll of a company of mounted volunteers, commanded by Capt. Holder Sisson, enrolled July 23, 1832, in Cook county, Illinois, for defense of northern portion of the State of Illinois, against the Sac and Fox Indians, and mustered out of service August 13, 1832:

Captain—Holder Sisson.

Lieutenants—First, Robert Stevens; Seccond, W. T. Bradford.

Sergeants—James Sayers, Uriah Wentworth, John Cooper, Abraham Francis.

Corporals—Armstead Runion, Thomas Coombs, Edward Poor, Cornelius C. VanHorn.

Privates—William Gougar, John Gougar, Nicholas Gougar, Daniel Gougar, Aaron Moore, Daniel Robb, Daniel Height, Aaron Friend, Joseph Norman, David Maggard, Aaron Wares, Thomas Francis, John McDeed, James McDeed, Abraham Van-Horn, Simon O. VanHorn, Wm. Rogers, Calvin Rowley, Selah Lanfear, David Crandall,· Alva Crandall, Daniel Mack, Wm. Barlow, Joseph Johnson, James Johnson, Silas Henderson, Patterson Frame, Oren Stevens, Joseph Cox, Alfred Johnson, Lucius Scott, Benjamin MacGard, Anderson Poor, Samuel Fleming, David Smith, Peter Lemesis, Timothy B. Clark, Barrett Clark, Wm. Clark, Enoch Darling, John Wilson, Wm. Chapman, O. L. Turner, James Mathews, Peter Lampseed.   Total, 60 men.

Of the DuPage and Naper Settlement Company we have not the dates of enrollment and muster out, but probably it would be about the same as in the other companies.

Captain—Joseph Naper.

Lieutenants—First, Alanson Sweet; Second, Sherman King.

Sergeants—First, S. M. Salsbury; Second, John Manning; Third, Walter Stowell; Fourth, John Naper.

Corporals—First, T. E. Parsons; Second, Lyman Butterfield; Third, I. P. Blodgett; Fourth, R. N. Murray.

Privates—P. F. W. Peck, William Barber, Richard W. Sweet, John Stevens, jr., Calvin M. Stowell, John Fox, Dennis Clark, Caleb Foster, Augustine Stowell, George Fox, T. Parsons, Daniel Landon, William Gault, Uriah Paine, John Stevens, Seth Westcott, Henry T. Wilson, Christopher Paine, Bailey Hobson, Josiah H. Giddings, Anson Ament, Calvin Ament, Edmund Harrison, Willard Scott, Percy Hawley, Peter Wickoff.

Of this last company, six, viz: Walter Stowell, I. P. Blodgett, Seth Westcott, Josiah H. Giddings, Willard Scott and Percy (or Pierce) Hawley, were from the present bounds of Will county.

In Captain Walker's company are some of the Fox river settlement, who had fled thither. The Second Lieutenant was of this number, who, no doubt, wanted revenge for the loss of his whisky and tobacco.

In Sisson's company there are several from the Walker's Grove or Plainfield Settlement, and some names which are entirely new to us. For the Naper and DuPage list we are indebted to Wm. Naper, a son of the Captain, and the list of the two other companies was kindly copied for us by our young friend Nat Rowell; the clerical force in the Adjutant-General's office at Washington being altogether inadequate to the herculean labor.

THE LAST OF SABBONEE.

Before closing our gleanings of fifty years ago we wish to say something more respecting Shabbonee, the white man's friend. After giving the settlers warning of the danger, as we have related, he, with his band of braves, joined the forces of Gen. Atkinson, and rendered important aid in the brief campaign, acting in the capacity of scouts

After the war (in 1833) a treaty was held at Chicago, by which the Pottawatamies disposed of their remaining lands to the United States, except some specific reservations to Caldwell, Robinson, Shabbonee and others, Indians and half-breeds. Two sections, including the grove, which Shabbonee for so many years made his home, were reserved to him. It was duly surveyed under direction of Major Langham, Surveyor-General of Illinois and Missouri at the time, and Shabbonee supposed that it was secured to him and heirs forever. In 1837, he accompanied his band, 130 in number, to their reservation in Missouri. He had been notified by the Indian agent that all of the band, except himself and family, must remove thither. He could not endure the thought of parting with his tribe, and therefore he accompanied them. But now he had to pay the penalty of his acts of friendship toward the white settlers in 1826 and 1832. The reservation of the Sacs and Foxes was very near that of the Pottawatamies. Black Hawk was still living, (he died October 3, 1838,) and he and his tribe cherished feelings of revenge against the white man's friend, the brave, by whose side he had fought for the English in 1812. No sooner had Shabbonee and his family reached their new home than a bitter warfare was commenced against them, which resulted in the death of his son, Pypagee, and of his nephew, Pyps, and in driving Shabbonee and the rest of his family back to Illinois. He narrowly escaped with his life from the vengeance of his Indian enemies.

Shabbonee and his family, about twenty in number, lived on his reservation in the grove which bears his name until 1849. At this time the Pottawatamies had been again removed to a new reservation in Kansas, and Shabbonee again sought with his family a home among them. He remained with them about three years, when he felt a strong desire to return again to his old home in DeKalb county. He fondly supposed that his rights would be respected by the people for whose safety he had incurred the deadly hatred of his red brethren. But on his reaching the beautiful grove, which he and his family had occupied for more than forty years, he found it in the possession of a stranger—that it was lost to him forever.

When the survey of the public lands lying north of the old Indian boundary was made the Deputy Surveyor, under instructions from the Land Department, ignored the former survey of the reservation, and included it in the regular section lines of the general U. S. survey, and during Shabbonee's absence in Kansas the land had been sold at public auction at Dixon.

When an appeal was afterwards made in Shabbonee's behalf to the Commissioner of the Land Department, the answer was returned that Shabbonee had forfeited and lost his title to the lands by leaving them. It is said that when he came to a full conviction of his forlorn condition, "albeit, all unused to the melting mood," he shed bitter tears. The brute who had got possession of his old home cursed him for having cut a few lodge poles in the grove which he thought was his own, and unfeelingly ordered him to leave the grove with his family. This he did, and never again visited it.

Let it be said to the credit of Ottawa that the citizens of that place raised a fund, bought him twenty acres of timber land on the Mazon, built him a comfortable house, and supplied him with means to start housekeeping again. Here he lived until his death, the 17th of July, 1859, in the 84th year of his age.

Gurdon S. Hubbard, who knew Shabbonee well, bears this testimony to his character: " From my first acquaintance with him, which began in the fall of 1818, to his death, I was impressed with the nobleness of his character, Physically, he was as fine a specimen of a man as I ever saw—tall, well proportioned, strong and active, with a face expressing great strength of mind and goodness of heart.

It is a curious fact that in the memorable Harrison campaign of 1840, there was published in the Chicago *Daily American*, a letter signed by "Chamblee," (Shabbonee) aid to Tecumseh," and " B. Caldwell, (Saug-a-nash) Captain," in which they contradict a campaign slander of Harrison's opponents, charging him with cowardice and inhumanity. This is dated at Council Bluffs, March 23, 1840. They say: "The first time we got acquainted with Gen. Harrison was at the council fire of Old Tempest, the

late Gen. Wayne, at his headquarters on the Wabash at Green-
ville, in 1796. From that time till 1811 we had many a friendly
smoke with him, but in 1812 we changed our tobacco smoke into
powder smoke. Then we found Gen. Harrison was a brave
warrior and humane to his prisoners," etc.

In 1861 a subscription was taken up in Ottawa, Morris and
other river towns, to erect a monument to Shabbonee, but
the breaking out of the war led to its abandonment. He was
buried with considerable public demonstration in the cemetery at
Morris, and only a plain marble slab points out where repose the
remains of THE WHITE MAN'S FRIEND.

The Black Hawk war, of which we have given a brief sketch
in the preceding pages, was not without its compensation. The
officers and soldiers who were sent to the aid of the settlers, and
who marched across our prairies and along our rivers carried
back with them glowing accounts of the beauty and fertility of
the country, which served to direct attention and emigration to
Northern Illinois, then the Far West, and almost a wilderness.
It is not easy to realize as one is whirled by the winged horse at
will by cultivated farms, past pleasant homes and through the
flourishing towns and cities that now cover this region, that fifty
years ago the few scattered settlers were fleeing from their log
cabins to escape the murderous raids of savage Indians. And as
one visits the great Briareus of the North-west, and sees how it
reaches with its giant arms two oceans, and gathers up the spoil
of many States, that fifty years ago were without a name,—how it
has covered with palace hotels, with cathedral churches, with great
warehouses and elevators, with miles on miles of compact, well-
built business blocks, and with beautiful villas, the low, wet
prairies and sloughs of fifty years ago,—it is hard, we say, for a

stranger to believe that at the period of which we have been writing, Chicago afforded but scant room, and poor protection to the few pioneer families that fled thither from the narrow circuit of forty miles. And yet there are still living some who can say, " Lo, our eyes have seen all this !"

JOLIET, August, 1882.

ERRATA.

On page 23, before the 10th line from bottom, these words should be supplied :—was concealed. Col. Henry

www.ingramcontent.com/pod-product-compliance
Lightning Source LLC
Chambersburg PA
CBHW022154020726
47496CB00008B/2709

* 9 7 8 3 3 3 7 0 1 4 3 5 3 *